RAINBOW GOSPEL

Report of the Conference on Challenging Racism in Britain sponsored by the Programme to Combat Racism of the World Council of Churches and the Community and Race Relations Unit of the British Council of Churches

All Saints Pastoral Centre, St Albans
October 1987

£1.50

ISBN 0-85169-173-0

© 1988. The British Council of Churches
Inter-Church House, 35-41 Lower Marsh, London, SE1 7RL.

Produced by Chippendale Press & Type, Otley, West Yorkshire.

Contents

Report Editors:
Kate Phillips and Revd David Haslam
Community and Race Relations Unit
British Council of Churches
35–41 Lower Marsh
London SE1 7RL

Introduction
Searching for Gold

Conferences are ephemeral things. Those planning the event spend weeks, months, even years, poring over speakers, programme, title and end-product. This report is part of the end-product of the conference on **Challenging Racism in Britain** which took place from 30 October to 1 November 1987, at the All Saints Pastoral Centre near St Albans, Hertfordshire. Other parts of that product include the experiences of the participants which they took away, the reports which many Christians read in the church media and the Declaration – of which 10,000 copies are being circulated. But this will be perhaps the most enduring product, and we hope that it will contribute to the vision of how the sin of racism is to be eliminated from our society. Such a vision is spiritual gold, the conference went looking for it and trusts that those reading the Report will join in the search.

The Community and Race Relations Unit (CRRU) of the British Council of Churches came into existence in 1971, partly as a result of the initiative of the World Council of Churches in setting up the Programme to Combat Racism (PCR) in 1969 and partly as a response by concerned Christians here in Britain over the growing visibility of racism in British Society. It has worked since then through educational programmes, the monitoring of racist trends, pressure on the churches to adopt more committed stances and – perhaps most effectively of all – through the Projects Fund, to challenge and combat racism in the United Kingdom.

The Programme to Combat Racism of the World Council of Churches came into being as a result of the Fourth Assembly of the Council in Uppsala in 1968. It has sought to expose racism at an international level and to side with the victims of oppression and exploitation wherever possible. Through its Special Fund it has supported those struggling against racism in all five continents, including Europe, and within Europe the United Kingdom. The PCR has challenged Christians to Christ's vision for humanity like no other church body this century – yet it has also been attacked and vilified, particularly for its grants to the liberation movements of Southern Africa, struggling against the most vicious system of racism since the Nazis. Because of these grants, some churches in Britain criticised the World Council, others reduced their financial contributions, one or two even resigned. Yet among the oppressed of the world the PCR is an agent of salvation.

Some saw in the attitude of the British churches to the Programme one of the clearest examples of British racism at the present time. It was to help the British churches to better understand the PCR, and perhaps to confront their own racism, that led to the concept of this conference.

The Planning Group of the conference was formed from BCC representatives, some of those responsible within the denominations for race issues, representatives from Christian anti-racist organisations and other co-optees. CRRU provided the servicing and co-ordination and inasmuch as there were faults should take the blame. The aims of the conference were as follows:-

To assess the causes, present patterns and effects of racism in British society;

To plan strategies for continuing anti-racist work both within and beyond the churches;

To raise the profile of PCR in the churches and the wider community;

To contribute to the agenda of CRRU as an instrument enabling the churches to effectively challenge racism in Britain.

The participants came from four main areas; there were nearly thirty representatives from member churches of the BCC, some twenty from black Christian organisations, a further thirty from anti-racist groups and movements at the base and around twenty-five others including the Planning Group, the representatives of the PCR and the Churches' Committee for Migrants in Europe, and some invited guests including Wilfred Wood, first black bishop in the Church of England.

The conference was structured around Working Groups on nine key areas in which racism seemed to the Planning Group to be at its most blatant. These are listed in the Working Group Section of the Report. To create the context for the groups, two keynote addresses were programmed with an additional contribution by Dr James Mutambirwa, Acting Director of the PCR. The first keynote speaker was Paul Boating, leading Methodist, Anglo-Ghanaian lawyer, Vice-Moderater of the PCR and one of the four black MPs elected in the May 1987 General Election. He was followed by Martin Mabiletsa, born in Alexandra township just outside Johannesburg, member of the Johannesburg Bar, exiled for his anti-apartheid activities, imprisoned for several months, now head of the Legal Representation Department at the Commission for Racial Equality. Both looked at racism in Britain from their different perspectives, while James Mutambirwa described an example of British racism in the response of our churches to the PCR, particularly its Special Fund.

After the groups had done their work, the Revd Dr Yvonne Delk of the United Church of Christ Church and Society Department in the USA and a member of the PCR Commission spoke on the black experience in the United States – both the pain and the inspiration. This provided the setting for the final sessions on amending and adding to the working group reports and finalising the Declaration which, after a descriptive preamble, drew on the group reports to produce a challenging list of recommendations for both Church and Government.

The ambience of the conference most felt to be positive. There were, however, criticism and disagreements. There was a clash in the opening session when a white speaker, not perhaps choosing words sufficiently carefully, provoked an angry reaction from some black participants. There was tension in at least one of the groups as whites challenged what they regarded as some of the sweeping generalisations in the opening speeches and requested chapter and verse. There was some defensiveness from those churches who suspended membership of the WCC over PCR activities. There was criticism from a North American black at the "breast-beating" of the victims and the "agonised silence" of the majority while failing to undertake the hard grind of strategising which had characterised the Civil Rights Movement in the United States. Old issues raised their heads yet again, one comment made was that if things are true we just have to go on saying them. New emphases appeared. Ultimately most participants seemed to feel it had been a mature conference, in which the strong tensions of earlier meetings had largely been left behind.

There was a reasonably good response in the Church media to the Declaration. Articles appeared in the Baptist Times, Methodist Recorder, Church Times, Catholic Herald, The Friend and The Tablet, with more modest snippets in Reform, The Universe and 21st Century Christian. The conference surfaced through the letter columns in Christian Week, but the only national paper to cover it was the Scotsman. Incidentally the word 'Black' in this report is normally understood to refer to people from Asia, Africa and the Caribbean. It is reproduced here with a small or capital B as the speakers or reporters themselves chose.

The final statement, being agreed at the All Saints Pastoral Centre, on All Saints Day, chose for itself the title **All Saints Declaration**. A participant afterwards remarked the title was primarily geographical and temporal but hopefully it contained a theological affirmation also.

Finally, this was a conference in which Black Christians demonstrated beyond all question that they have arrived at the heart of the British Church and that they have an irreplaceable contribution to make. There was a confidence in themselves and their message for the traditional and almost entirely white-led churches which some white participants seemed to find a little threatening, and a few left early, but which most welcomed – recognising that church life could never now be the same.

Rainbow Gospel? The conference elicited this description in two crucial ways. It demonstrated the colourful, multi-racial, multi-cultural society Britain has now become, and it manifested that promise of God announced in Genesis Chapter 9, in which God makes his covenant, not with human or animal, not with black or white, but "between myself and all that lives on earth", (Genesis 9, 17 NEB). And the symbol of that covenant –

My bow I set in the cloud
Sign of the covenant
Between myself and earth.

And at the end of the rainbow? Spiritual gold!

Revd. David Haslam

5

Racism in Britain Today
Paul Boateng

We come together to share the issue of the struggle against racism in modern Britain.

We have to recognise the nature of racism, the way in which it has pervaded our country for very many years, the way in which Britain has had as one of its major exports racism, second only to religion as an export to the rest of the world. Racism scars our country and scars the world; racism represents, for those of us who are Christian, a gaping wound in the body of Christ. As Christians we have come together with non-Christians who are acting in the struggle against racism. We seek to develop a strategy to combat racism, to promote a successful multi-racial society in this country and to address those global issues which relate to our own struggle in this country. That is why the contributions of our sisters and brothers from all over the world – Southern Africa, United States, Africa, are so important.

Immigration and Nationality Law

We need to address our particular situation in Britain at this time. This gathering takes place on the eve of the introduction of a new Immigration Bill into Parliament. One of the characteristics of race relations in our country is the way in which the context of those relations has been set by the law in relation to immigration and nationality. Racism in Britain is enshrined in these laws. The concept of patriality by descent is a racist concept. The nationality and immigration laws are designed to exclude black people, to present them as a problem in themselves, so that we as black people become the problem not racism.

You can pass all the acts for race relations in the world, you can have a Commission for Racial Equality, you can give people leadership and resources, you can have countless black Members of Parliament, but so long as those laws are on the statute book then the context of race relations in this country is fundamentally racist. So the removal of the racism of the nationality and immigration laws must be a primary target for the community and the church in Britain at this time.

We must therefore examine a strategy to oppose the Immigration Bill, and also to secure the future of Commonwealth citizens affected by the deadline that falls on 31 December, 1987. This gathering will have failed unless at the end we have some way forward for the churches and community in these matters.

Racial Violence

The immigration and nationality laws continue to present blacks as the problem. And if it is still possible for senior British politicians – for even the Prime Minister – to talk in terms of this country being 'swamped' by other cultures, then why should we be surprised that the Asian woman in Tower Hamlets gets chased home, that the youngster in Birmingham gets his head kicked in, that the individual alone in Walthamstow wakes up one night to find petrol in the front room, to find the door to the house alight, to find the windows broken, to find the shop broken into again? Because after all the people who are doing those things are doing no more than giving vent to a sentiment that is quite clearly understood, and accepted. "Enough is enough, there are too many of them, if we encourage some to go then we are doing a public service."

We underwrite that sort of attitude when we continue to present the mere existence of black people as a problem. It creates in black youth a sense of alienation, a rootlessness, which manifests itself in a variety of ways. It eats away at their capacity to enhance their own life, it creates a real crisis of identity for all too many of our people.

Black people are still – in relation to many in the Christian churches – people who live somewhere over there, in the inner cities, who live somewhere else. "Racism isn't a problem in our church – we have no blacks". That is the reality of church life in many parishes. We need to recognise that we live in a multi-racial society even though we may live in Devon, Mid-Wales or Northumbria. We are educating young people in a world in which as never before, they will come into contact with people of different races and cultures. If we fail to do this adequately violence results.

Education Legislation

The new Education Bill creates an important debate here. The churches and the community must play their role. The development of the 'core curriculum' must be on our agenda. Let us make sure the Church uses its role to address the issues – the multi-cultural nature of education, religious education, and parental 'choice' as well as the core curriculum.

The Right to Resources and the Poll Tax

There is a sense of self-confidence in the community now that did not exist a decade ago. It has happened because communities in struggle have responded to adverse circumstances, have formed alliances with people of other races, of other faiths, have been prepared to come together.

We have to build on that, particularly at a time when the resources that helped fuel that process, have either gone or are in the process of going. Once people have started down the road that enables them to power then nothing can stop them. We have to see that at this time of attack on public funding and the right of communities to influence and determine what local priorities should be.

Worse than the loss of resources our very right to influence the political process is threatened with the Poll Tax. We may on a massive scale be disenfranchised. In America they fought a bitter battle against Poll Tax. They had to strike down linking of the payment of taxes with the right to vote. Imagine what it is going to be like, persuading people on some of the great estates, some of our most depressed and run-down areas, to put their names to a piece of paper that will mean them having to pay a lot of money. And Thatcher is going to make sure that areas served by some of our wealthiest congregations don't have to pay, they'll be paying less than ever before. And Christians must recognise how this kind of political process cries out for our involvement.

The role of the Bishops, and of the Church and its capacity to lobby and to organise, is going to be absolutely vital. We are going to have to support each other in that process, because if we don't we are going to find ourselves denied the power and resources that are ours by right. And the importance of a gathering like this is the way in which that interdependence is worked out. There is also the practical question of the way the churches are relating to the communities in which they serve. This is a 'bricks and mortar' matter, how we share the buildings we possess.

Sharing Church Buildings

When it comes to actually sharing on the High Street, what happens if we have to sell our buildings? If it is a choice between a carpet retail outlet and a growing and vibrant black church; who will win? Whoever provides the most money; and all too often it is the carpet store. And that is the fate of many of our churches; they become carpet warehouses, or places where stripped-pine furniture is dispensed to a waiting gentrified area, when there are black churches, communities of Christians, crying out for resources. Now surely it is not beyond the Church to find some way of organising our affairs to enable those resources to be shared.

At a time when all too many grass-root activist groups are seeking to provide services for young mothers, mentally-handicapped people, youth groups for whom the council can no longer provide, there must be a way that churches, who have property, can find some way of sharing.

Mental Health

I want to take the issue of mental health and black people as being a critical issue, and one which we must bring to the fore as we have not been able to do before. Mental health is a critical issue, people suffering from mental illness are not easy to work with. It is not easy for us as black people to go out into the world and say we have a mental health problem, when our whole community is being dismissed as pathological.

It is a problem that addresses itself in every part of our community, Africans, Asians, Afro-Caribbeans. The issue of youth; if you go to some of our mental hospitals, there are so many young people. We have to do something about it, to demand that action is taken. For a long time there was no such thing as family therapy in relation to blacks. Blacks were deemed incapable of benefitting from family therapy – the reason being of course that the black family was pathological.

We need to make community care effective – we are not saying that black people should not be sent to mental institutions – it is a question of saying that both black and white people should have appropriate treatment. I intend to seek an adjournment motion on this matter and the House of Commons will have to consider what it is prepared to do about it.

The Immigration Bill

There are going to be four main changes introduced into immigration legislation in Parliament in 1988: first there is the imposition of new procedures that will speed up the removal of overstayers; this will mean a curtailment, still further, of possible avenues of appeal to the Courts because the Home Secretary has not had happy experiences of late in Courts. So Government is trying to remove these matters from their jurisdiction.

Then there is the issue of polygamous marriages; the numbers involved are very small, hardly twenty every year. But you can imagine what certain of our newspapers will make of the issue of polygamy, if they somehow find one of those twenty. The whole of black family life will once again be stereotyped as being heathen and pathological.

Third comes a reduction in the right of appeal in this country of people who come to the country and maintain that they have the right to remain by virtue of their descent. I can tell you from personal experience, of one particular case of someone from Sri Lanka. There is no way that we would have been able to establish whether this woman was entitled by virtue of patriality to remain had we not been able to obtain – because she was *here* – access to records and documentation.

Finally, and in some ways worst of all, there is a change in section one sub-section five of the Immigration Act 1971, in relation to the right of parents to bring their dependents, wives and children into this country. A provision now is to be introduced which will require a person to show that they are able to be in a position to support their dependent wives and children "without recourse to public funds". That means that unless you are a beneficiary of Thatcher's economic largesse, then you can forget about bringing a dependent wife and children to this country.

The Global Context

Those of us who call ourselves Christian have a prophetic duty to undertake as far as we are able the task of transforming the world. That is our responsibility. That is part of our faith-journey, making our faith real. It was James who in effect said "Faith is action."

I ask anyone who examines the history of Africa and the Indian sub-continent and the history of our liberation, for example the recent history of Zimbabwe, "Who is in the forefront of the struggle?" It is men and women of spiritual power! If you look at those places in the world where the confrontation is between those who seek to exploit and those who seek to liberate, there it is most acute. If you look at the Caribbean and Latin America and that arena of struggle, who are in the forefront there? Christians are in the forefront there, side by side with all those seeking to bring about a transformation.

In today's Britain black people have to know exactly where we are going and how we intend to apply ourselves, and not try and explain or apologise for those aspects of our past that are shameful. We need now to look to our present and look to our future, and that is the task of this conference. I urge you to join me in this task.

Racism in Britain – a South African Perspective
by Martin Mabiletsa

The Roots of Racism

The most devastating experience for a South African exile arriving in his country of choice for asylum is the explosion in his face of all the illusions that he has entertained about the 'mother of democracy'. For me this was an immediate experience for my family and I were settled in Handsworth, Birmingham. I was immediately struck by the massive unemployment of Black people, the horrid conditions of their housing, the high rate of illiteracy or bare literacy and the hostility of some members of the police force. This was a rather traumatic experience to find that just as in South Africa we were afraid of moving about at night lest some bored policeman would find us an object of entertainment under the notorious 'sus' laws which seem about to be re-introduced. In that area very Black people who had been arrested had not been charged under this law.

Because of this power of the police and its unscrupulous usage, a tremendous tension had developed by the time of our arrival in 1979. I was not surprised when the inner city explosions of 1981 took place. I think it is ill-advised to re-introduce this law in the Criminal Justice Bill. I believe that opposition to its re-introduction must be given immediate priority.

Racism is alive and prospering in Great Britain. As the Policy Studies Institute have pointed out in their research "Racial Discrimination: Seventeen Years After the Act" racism has intensified instead of abating. I do not believe that we can begin to address the problem of racism unless we understand its ideological basis. There are numerous views about what racism is. But the most commonly-held is one expressed by the Rampton Inquiry into the Education of Children from Ethnic Minority Groups. They state in their report *"In our view racism describes a set of attitudes and behaviour towards people of another race which is based on the belief that races are distinct and can be graded as "superior" or "inferior". A racist is therefore someone who believes that people of a particular race, colour or national origin are inherently inferior, so that their identity, culture, self-esteem, views and feelings are of less value than his or her own and can be disregarded or treated as less important".*

I do not disagree with this definition but find it incomplete. In my view racism is simply an instrument of oppression for there is no scientific or reasoned basis for the belief that any race is superior to another. Racism has always been practised by those who know better. The Third Reich knew that the Jews were not inferior just as those responsible for the institutionalised racism against Black people in this country know that they are not inferior. In South Africa they had to pass the Bantu Education Act in 1953 because they realised that Black people were beginning to excel the whites even though their educational facilities were inferior.

Racial prejudice in Britain is as old as the hills. Elizabeth I was the first to express disquiet about the large numbers of black people in Britain during her reign. These sentiments persisted through to the Victorian era. Indeed from time to time the black numbers in London were reduced by repatriation. However, no racist violence is recorded until immediately after the First World War when black soldiers and seamen who had fought for King and country came back home and found workers' associations implacably opposed to the employment of black seamen when white crews were available. Seven weeks after the end of the war William P Samuels from British Guiana, a seaman stranded in Cardiff, wrote to the Colonial Office:

"We kindly beg to appeal to you for justice. We are seafaring men that has served this country faithfully in her past difficulties either in the services of His Britannic Majesty or in the Mercantile Marine . . . We do not want any favour, all we want is fair play. Every morning we go down to shipping offices to find ourselves work so as to make an honest bread and are bluntly refused on account of our colour. Whereas, foreigners of all nationality get the preference. This is not only in Cardiff but throughout the United Kingdom".

A series of incidents of this kind of racial victimisation led to the so called race riots of Liverpool and Cardiff. A typical incident was the one that involved Black seamen (Arabs, Somalis, West African and African Caribbeans) who had settled in South and North Shields in the 1860s. In February 1919 some Arab seamen, all British subjects, having paid £1 each to clear their union books, which had to be up to date before they could ship out, were then refused work. When they objected, the shop steward incited a crowd of foreign white seamen against them. The black victims were later arrested and most sentenced to terms of imprisonment. The police had acted against the victims. This was to be the pattern in all those riots. Black people began to identify the police as the enemy.

Present Issues

I have cited these historical examples because, as you are aware, almost every inquiry into the recent inner city disturbances has identified two views which have been forcefully articulated by the black community – police harassment and the deep frustration that goes with deprivation.

There is an enormous 60 – 70% unemployment amongst Black people. The PSI report states that the white applicant is over a third more likely to receive a positive response from the employer than are black applicants.

At least a third of the employers covered in the study are unlawfully discriminatory. It also found that black applicants who had been discriminated against would have no evidence to suggest that it had happened. What is curious is that even the theoretical foundations for this most pernicious disease have not changed since 1919. At the height of the 1919 race riots in Liverpool the Liverpool Courier in an editorial headed "Black and White" wrote: *"One of the chief reasons of popular anger behind the present disturbances lies in the fact that the average negro is nearer the animal than is the average white man . . . The white man regards (the Black man) as part-child, part-animal and part-savage." It is true that many of the blacks in Liverpool are of a low type, that they insult and threaten respectable women in the street, and that they are invariably unpleasant and provocative."*

Even as I was reading this article I thought of the racist hysteria in the gutter press after Brixton, Handsworth and more recently Tottenham. I thought of the shamelessly evil attacks on Bernie Grant, one of the most outstanding leaders in our community – black or white. I thought of the concerted attacks by the same media against Black-led councils which have been represented as 'looney' because of their courage to address the question of Equal Opportunities. I cannot pretend that I agree with everything they have done but they must be admired for their contribution.

Maureen Cain in her book *Society and the Policeman's Role* (1973) and Joseph Hunte's report to the West Indian Standing Conference published as *'Nigger-Hunting in England'* (1966); showed how racism had become a key component of policemen's occupational culture. Cain found that policemen generally believed that "niggers in the main are pimps, layabouts, living off what we pay in taxes . . . They are different, separate and incomprehensible. There was, therefore, no good reason for not being violent if the occasion arose".

This research is confirmed by the recent experience of John Fernandes, a black ex-lecturer at the Hendon Police College, who found an all-pervasive racism amongst the young recruits. Home Office research confirms that there are racist elements in the police force. That is why it has become a bad joke for Black people to summon the police when they are racially harassed or attacked.

In parliament white racism and violence has been blamed on the Black presence. The fewer Black people there are in this country the better it would be for race relations. There is a continuum of opinion from Powellism which advocates repatriation to a Roy Hattersley who said in 1965 'without limitation integration is impossible, without integration limitation is unacceptable'. Now we have another Immigration Bill designed to limit the numbers of black people here.

At the educational level the Rampton Inquiry found that African-Caribbean children were under-achieving partly because whites feel that they are unlikely to achieve in academic terms but may have high expectations of their potential in areas such as sport, dance and art". Teachers regard these children as pupils who inevitably caused difficulties and tend to refer to these British-born children as "them" and "those people", or as "immigrants".

In a recent investigation on suspension in Birmingham the Commission for Racial Equality found that almost invariably the chances of suspension of black pupils were four to five times higher than their white counterparts for similar incidents. Black pupils were kept for longer periods in the remedial schools than white children.

In South Africa through the Bantu Education Act 1953 our educational system was emasculated. The apartheid regime intended Black people to be educated only to a level where they could serve the white masters. The African National Congress' efforts to establish an alternative education were outlawed and the schools that had been established were ruthlessly suppressed with the customary police brutality. We succumbed. But the battle was carried into the classroom. Black teachers educated Black children beyond Bantu Education. Although we couldn't completely overcome, I am proud to say that we do have some Black doctors and consultants and professionals in Soweto and elsewhere. We have students at universities. That is the reason why the apartheid regime provoked the present crisis that has kept our children out of the classroom since June, 1976.

Black Resistance

Black people in the United Kingdom do not have an even chance of fighting from within. But I am proud to observe that up and down the country there is a fight-back. Supplementary and summer schools are being established all over the country. And, like in the USA where Black people suffered similar oppression, the Black churches are beginning to establish schools that are free from racist oppression that undermines the Black pupils' confidence. The result is that under-achievement will soon be a thing of the past. A shining example is the Seventh Day Adventist School in London where passing A-levels presents no difficulties to Black children.

I want to say to those delegates who represent the Black Churches here that I have first-hand experience of this struggle for I am the grandson of Paulos Marthinus Mabiletsa who broke away from the Lutheran Church as a result of racism to set up the Christian Apostolic Church in Zion in the early part of this century in Alexandra. He was a man of vision who fervently believed that a people without education are a lost people. He therefore built a primary school and a high school in Alexandra township which had free board and lodging for the poor pupils

Racism and the Church

It is because of this background that I was curious to find out what role the established church plays here. I was struck by an old GLC poster which said *"What colour are you my God? There is racism in the church too."* This increased my curiosity. I therefore began to scrutinize the Anglican and Roman Catholic churches which I recognized as the dominant churches in this country and found that there were hardly any Black clergy.

I was then curious to examine how these churches treated the picture of the Black Madonna and Child which is a presentation of Jesus Christ and his mother as Black people, and also the Black saints and popes – like Gelasius I – the 49th pope after Saint Peter who was born of African parents and was renowned all over the world for his learning and holiness. I could not find the Black Madonna and Child in all the churches I went to in London. I then went to Canterbury Cathedral and after a thorough search found the Black Madonna and Child displayed in an obscure corner in the basement of the church.

I began to examine the history of racism in this country and have found no evidence that when Black people were under racist attack, from 1919 up until now, they have received protection or solace from the church. There was no evidence that the church had tried to awaken the consciences of its children to this abominable illogical evil that has claimed millions of lives over the centuries and is now responsible for the murder of Black families.

I began to think of the doctrinal foundations of apartheid. In South Africa apartheid finds credence by what has been called "Jehovah and Noah's curse that created Negroes." *"Now I cannot beget the fourth son whose children I would have ordered to serve you and your brothers! Therefore it must be Canaan, your first-born, whom they enslave. And since you have disabled me doing ugly things in the blackness of night, Canaan's children shall be born black: Moreover, because you twisted your head around to see my nakedness, your grand-children's hair shall be twisted into kinks, and their eyes red again; because your lips jested at my misfortune, theirs shall swell, and because you neglected my nakedness, they shall go naked, and their male members shall be shamefully elongated; Men of this race are called Negroes, their forefather Canaan commanded them to love theft and fornication, to be banded together in hatred of their masters and never to tell the truth!"*

(*Blacks and Jews: an Old Confrontation*, Prof Yosef A A Ben-Jochannan)

This is the doctrine of the Dutch Reformed Church of South Africa. As you are aware this doctrine had no scriptural foundation.

I also began to think of the Resolution on Religion of The Seventh International Convention of The Negro Peoples of The World held under the auspices of the Universal Negro Improvement Association in August 1934 in Kingston, Jamaica. UNIA was the organisation founded by Marcus Mosiah Garvey whose centenary is being celebrated this year. That resolution reads: *"That we implore members of the race to acquire an intelligent conception of the God they worship, as well as an intelligent interpretation of the Bible and other recognised religious textbooks; that Negroes make their religion a fountain of inspiration rather than a valley of tears, lamentation and fear; that members of the race conceive their Deity as a Spirit not foreign to their own creation but akin to it; that when it becomes necessary – as is the traditional religious practice – to think of the Deity in physical form, his image and likeness be dramatized in the physical beauty and characteristics of the Negro himself."*

This resolution was inspired by Garvey because in his sojourn in Europe and the USA he had found that religion was used as an instrument for the physical and mental enslavement of Black people. The Church must combat any bias in religious representation that seeks to inculcate an inferiority complex in Black people.

In conclusion, I believe that the starting point for combating racism must be within the church itself. The church must begin to address its own employment and equal opportunities policies in relation to Black people in this country. Only when the church is truly multi-racial in its composition and non-racial in its doctrinal approach will it begin to have relevance to the Black experience.

I am sure that throughout the centuries religion has been and still is the most powerful influence on humanity. I believe that influence from the pulpit can be used to combat racist thinking and practice amongst those who control our lives and I believe that this influence can be used to convert ordinary folk as well. I find it tragic that Black people felt so unwelcome in the established churches that they had to establish their own.

Now the Church must join with Black people to fight against racism in schools, employment, housing, policing and other areas. The established church has a powerful voice in the House of Lords. It should use this influence to challenge legislation which discriminates in any way against black people.

Racism in Britain: a PCR View

James Mutambirwa

The WCC has, since its formation in 1948, always strongly condemned racism. The First Assembly of the WCC which met in Amsterdam in 1948 said: the Church "must call society away from prejudice based upon race or colour and from the practices of discrimination and segregation as denials of justice and human dignity . . ." And against racist actions of governments "the churches must take a firm and vigorous stand, through local action, in cooperation with churches in other lands, and through international institutions of legal order."

Again in 1954 the Evanston Assembly addressed the issue of racism. "The problems of race, difficult as they are, insoluble as they sometimes appear to be, provide for Christians an opportunity for obedience, and for a deeper understanding that bond and free, Jew and Gentile, Greek and Barbarian, people of every land and continent, are all one in Christ." The 1961 Third New Delhi Assembly called upon the churches to actively join in the struggle against racial oppression. The Assembly declared "where oppression, discrimination and segregation exist, the churches should identify themselves with the oppressed race in its struggle to achieve justice. Christians should be ready to lead in this struggle." And in Nairobi in 1975, the Fifth Assembly denounced "racism as a sin against God and against fellow human beings."

Though the WCC made many statements against racism it seemed inadequate in enabling the churches to face the challenge that racism posed for them and society; little changed. In 1966 the World Conference on Church and Society which met in Geneva said "It is not enough for churches and groups to condemn the sin of racial arrogance and oppression. The struggle for radical change in structures will inevitably bring suffering and will demand costly and bitter engagement. For Christians to stand aloof from this struggle is to be disobedient to the call of God in history. The meaning of the Cross for our time can be nothing less than this." In 1968 the Fourth Assembly warned. "Contemporary racism robs all human rights of their meaning, and is an imminent danger to world peace."

But all these statements did not bring any change in society. The 1960s in Africa were characterised by the struggle against racism and colonial rule and in the United States the civil rights struggle led by Dr Martin Luther King Jr was a struggle against racism and for equality and human dignity. The black power movement of the 1960s led by Rap Brown, Stokely Carmichael and the Black Muslims' spokesman Malcolm X – all attacked racism in the United States. The fact that the churches were asked to pay reparations to the blacks for all they had suffered over three hundred years of American history showed that the Church was still a racist institution. The black power movement of the 1960s in the United States had echoes in the United Kingdom in Tariq Ali and others.

After a WCC-sponsored consultation on racism in London in 1969, the WCC formed a new sub-unit, the Programme to Combat Racism (PCR) to specifically and actively fight against racism. PCR has since become the instrument of the WCC to fight against racism the world over, and in particular apartheid in South Africa.

PCR fights racism in Germany where the Turks are discriminated against. Germans deny that there is racism in their country. To many Germans racism 'means' or is 'associated' with nazism. Dislike of Turks and discrimination against them is called xenophobia. The rise of Le Pen and his National Front in France shows that racism is far from dead in that country. PCR is also involved in the struggle against racism in North and South America. The population of Brazil is 55% black, but this is not reflected in the government, universities, trade unions or even in the Church.

During a PCR visit to Brazil we asked a catholic bishop why there were so few black priests and bishops in the church. He replied that "priests and bishops are called to the priesthood. The church does not go out to recruit priests." I replied, "It is very interesting that in Africa before independence not too many Africans were called to be bishops but after independence many were called and are still being called to serve God." We asked him why in the offices of the diocese there were neither black secretaries nor even cleaners.

In a conversation with a black group in Brasilia we were told the story of a black sociologist who while lecturing to a mostly white class was surprised when one of his white students said that blacks were lazy, they were not clever, they steal – the usual racial stereotypes. The white students were surprised when the sociologist said, "How can you say such things, I am black". The sociologist was in turn surprised when the student said, "But you are not black." In Brazil if you are successful, you cease to be black in the eyes of the whites.

In Japan, PCR is involved in the fight against discrimination of the Koreans and the Buraku, by Japanese society. The Koreans, even those born in Japan, are considered aliens and are discriminated against in education, employment and housing. The Buraku are despised and treated as second class citizens who experience discrimination at every level of Japanese society.

PCR is also active in fighting against racism in New Zealand where the Maoris suffer discrimination. In Australia we support the struggle by the Aborigines against racism and degradation, and for their land-rights; similarly the indigenous people in North and South America.

So PCR has a global programme against racism. We also are concerned about racism in the United Kingdom. When you read British newspapers you realise that racism is alive and well in Britain. I remember very well Powell's famous speech about the danger of rivers of blood unless blacks in Britain were repatriated. Today the fear of white Britain being 'swamped' by blacks from Asia, the Caribbean and Africa is expressed, not even subtly, in the tough immigration laws now being proposed in Parliament.

Educational and medical facilities for the blacks are poor, also housing. Unemployment among the blacks is very high. In the sensational press the blacks are portrayed negatively. What is the Church doing? How is it challenging racism in Britain today?

Between 1970 and 1987 the World Council of Churches gave $464,000 to groups of the racially-oppressed in Britain and to groups that support them but in the same period received contributions to the Special Fund totalling just $92,014 from British Christians.

A grant from the Special Fund is, in a very symbolic way, a way of empowering the oppressed. Grants are also made to those groups that assist the racially-oppressed. The aim of a Special Fund grant is to strengthen the organisational capacity of those suffering under racial oppression. In 1969 the WCC called the churches "to move beyond charity, grants and traditional programming to relevant and sacrificial action leading to new relationships of dignity and justice among all and to become agents for the radical reconstruction of society."

So why do the churches in Britain contribute so little to the Special Fund? In 1985 the US churches contributed a miserable $2,500. Why? There are several reasons. The churches in Britain and the US reflect their societies which are racist. The churches are not comfortable at all with the Special Fund grants to the liberation movements in Southern Africa. Grants to the African National Congress (ANC), the South West African People's Organisation (SWAPO) and the Pan Africanist Congress (PAC) are seen as grants to terrorist organisations that use 'violence' in their struggle to dismantle apartheid. Many church people in the West believe that the money given to the liberation movements is used to buy guns. In 1986 the ANC received $80,000 from the Special Fund. The ANC looks after over twenty thousand refugees in Tanzania, Zambia, Zimbabwe and Angola. So the WCC Special Fund contributes $4 to each refugee. The Special Fund is given to the liberation movements for humanitarian purposes. An upper middle class family of four in the US finds it difficult to make ends meet on a salary of $80,000 a year. Yet a grant of $4 to a South African refugee causes a big uproar in the CBS *Sixty Minutes* program and in the *Readers Digest*. Is this not racism – to suggest or imply that $4 is too much for a black refugee?

Western churches do not like to be reminded of the racism in their society and in their own house. Why is it that the PCR and the Special Fund are applauded in Southern Africa – the whole of Africa – and by the majority of blacks in the United States and in Britain? The fund is seen by blacks as the visible symbolic act of solidarity by the over 300 member churches of the WCC. To millions of blacks around the world PCR is the conscience of the church.

The churches in Britain do not support the Special Fund because they are not the 'agents for radical reconstruction of society' for which the WCC called in 1969. Between 1970 and 1987 the British churches contributed only $92,000 to the PCR. Perhaps they were giving their money to black organisations fighting racism in Britain. Well, were they? *(See the tables for grants to and from Britain 1970 to 1987)*

Donations from and grants to Europe 1970 – 1986 (Grants 1987 included)

| | US Dollars | |
	Donations	Grants
Austria	5	13.000
Belgium	73.436	83.000
Denmark	12.037	–
Federal Republic of Germany	1.500.009	127.000
Finland	12.646	6.000
France	7.623	398.500
German Democratic Republic	39.948	–
Greece	19.783	–
Ireland	2	22.000
Italy	7.073	7.500
Liechtenstein	31	–
Luxembourg	54	–
Netherlands	233.594	82.000
Norway	303.186	3.500
Portugal	–	4.000
Sweden	847.576	–
Switzerland	204.178	44.500
United Kingdom	85.474	464.000
Totals 1970 – 1986 (1987)	**$3.346.655**	**1.255.000**

(Donations received in 1987 in total $297.010)

Sources of Income for the Special Fund to Combat Racism of WCC/PCR
1969 – 1987 (US Dollars)

UNITED KINGDOM

1970	Methodist Missionary Society	1.200	
	3 gifts	36	1.236
1971	Iona Community	120	
	Greenbank Church, Edinburgh	497	
	3 gifts	35	652
1972	Methodist Missionary Society	1.302	
	Iona Community	260	
	Special Appeal (141 gifts)	3.149	4.711
1973	Iona Community	246	
	Methodist Missionary Society	2.412	
	Methodist Relief Fund	913	
	gifts via Ms P Webb	137	
	Methodist Church	809	
	25 gifts	536	5.053
1974	Methodist Missionary Society	2.388	
	Methodist Relief Fund	1.172	
	Iona Community	237	
	Tax Refund on UK Donations 1974	1.074	
	28 gifts	613	5.484
1975	Iona Community	4.296	
	via Methodist Church	744	5.040
1976	Methodist Church	1.943	
	26 gifts	843	2.786
1977	Methodist Church	2.638	
	9 gifts	255	2.893
1978	Methodist Church	4.151	
	via British Council of Churches	1.710	
	10 gifts	1.575	7.436
1979	Methodist Church (DSR)	5.350	
	via British Council of Churches	1.998	
	8 gifts	1.270	8.618
1980	Methodist Church/DSR	5.901	
	Methodist Church/OD	164	
	3 gifts	680	6.745
1981	British Council of Churches	19.788	
	Methodist Church	804	
	Various gifts	556	21.148
1982	Various gifts		2.065

1983	British Council of Churches	2.940	
	1 gift	8	2.948
1984	British Council of Churches	1.090	
	Methodist Church	1.495	
	Ecumenical Parish, Stanton	281	
	Ecumenical Parish, Stanton	281	
	Individual gifts (6)	535	3.401
1985	Methodist Church	3.352	
	Individual gifts (2)	150	3.502
1986	Methodist Church	1.517	
	Individual gifts (2)	239	1.756
1987	Methodist Church	4.602	
	United Reformed Church	10	
	Individual gifts (8)	1.928	6.540
Total United Kingdom			**$92.014**

Grants approved by the Executive Committee of the World Council of Churches from 1970–1987

United Kingdom	US Dollars
Africa Bureau – 1970	2.500.--
All Faiths For One Race	6.000.--
Anti-apartheid Movement – 1970, 73, 74, 75, 76, 77, 78, 79, 80, 83	54.500.--
Association of Black Clergy – 1987	6.000.--
Committee for Freedom in Mozambique, Angola and Guinea – 1974	4.000.--
Europe Third World Research Project – 1971, 74	7.500.--
Free University for Black Studies – 1971	2.500.--
Hong-Kong Research Project – 1977, 80	17.500.--
Institute of Race Relations – 1973, 75, 76, 77, 79, 80, 81, 82	73.000.--
International Defence and Aid Fund – 1970	3.000.--
Joint Council for the Welfare of Immigrants – 1977, 78, 79, 80, 81, 84	54.000.--
Liverpool 8 Law Centre – 1982	4.000.--
Migrants Action Group – 1982, 86, 87	14.000.--
Namibia Communications Centre – 1985, 86, 87	9.500.--
Namibia Support Committee – 1978, 79	10.000.--
Race Today Collective – 1974, 76, 77 78, 79, 80, 81	111.500.--
Searchlight – 1981, 82, 83	16.500.--
South African Non-Racial Olympic Committee – 1981	5.000.--
Southall Monitoring Group – 1986, 87	6.000.--
Southall Rights – 1983, 84, 85	12.000.--
Southall Youth Movement – 1980, 81, 82	25.500.--
Wales Anti-Apartheid Movement – 1984, 85, 86, 87	12.000.--
West Indian Standing Conference – 1970	7.500.--
Total grants approved for United Kingdom	**$464.000.--**

Racism: a Perspective from the United States

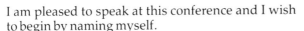

Yvonne V Delk, Executive Director of the Office for Church in Society, United Church of Christ, USA

I am pleased to speak at this conference and I wish to begin by naming myself.

I am an African American. Three hundred and eighty six years ago, a Dutch ship landed twenty Africans at Jamestown, Virginia in the United States of America to begin an incomplete chapter in the history of civilization. I am the descendant of those mothers and fathers who experienced whips, chains, slave ships, auction blocks, plantations, Ku Klux Klan lynchings, 'separate but equal' laws, bus boycotts, picket lines, hoses, jails and the racist philosophy of law and order.

I am a Spiritual Person. I am a minister of the Gospel of Jesus Christ and I am a daughter of the Black Church. It was there that my mother and father brought my six brothers and sisters and myself in order that we could receive value and meaning as members of the household of God and of faith. Through the week my parents were considered by the predominant culture to be objects. They were nothings and nobodies, but on Sunday they were Sister Delk and Brother Delk bound together with other sisters and brothers in the Black Church as an extended family.

The Black Church equipped me with a faith, the courage to resist oppression, and love to lift me and my sisters and brothers from bondage into freedom. It was there that I came to love and embrace the God of Justice, the God who sides with the poor and the oppressed. Everything that I am as well as what I ought to be was shaped in the context of the Black Church.

I am a person who believes that the Gospel speaks to the liberation, redemption, and renewal of persons, institutions and nations. I believe that time and time again we are called to lay down our lives for the sake of the gospel. We are called to do more than oppose evil, we must resist it by speaking truth to power, engaging in actions that seek to transform and humanize our globe.

I am pleased that I am asked to share *a* perspective on racism from the position of one who lives in the United States of America. This is not a definitive statement. While the victims of racism represent the rainbow of colours within the United States, I will not be speaking from the perspective of Native American sisters and brothers who have not only known slavery, poverty and political conquest; they have known something else - genocide. Their experience and story reveals one of the greatest mass exterminations of any race or culture. The numbers are so large that we have lost our ability to name or to remember them. Neither will I be representing the experience of sisters and brothers who are Hispanic and Asian. They came to the new world looking for new opportunities and instead found a nightmare of racism. *I will simply share my perspective.*

My perspective is informed in part by a celebration that is occurring in our nation. 1987 marks the two hundredth anniversary of the Constitution of the United States of America.

I choose to celebrate by being in this place joining sisters and brothers who offer a more inclusive view of the world. I do not believe the wisdom, foresight, and sense of justice exhibited by the framers of the Constitution particularly profound. To the contrary, the Government that they devised was defective from the start, requiring several amendments, a civil war and numerous social transformations to attain the system of constitutional government and its respect for the individual freedoms and human rights that we hold as fundamental today.

The first words of the Constitution preamble are "We the People." When the founding fathers used this phrase in 1787, they did not have in mind the majority of America's citizens. "We the People" included only free persons. African slaves were excluded, Native Americans were excluded, and women did not gain the right to vote for over a hundred and fifty years. The concept of "we the people" was therefore corrupt from the beginning because it was exclusive. It referred to a white society that was founded upon the extermination of one race and the enslavement of another. *Racism is therefore deeply rooted in the American society.* It is sustained in 1987 by both personal attitudes and structural forces. In order to move deeper into this analysis, I offer you a parable, two affirmations and a challenge.

The Parable

A girl was walking down the street with a cage which contained a bird. As she walked with the cage and the bird, she prodded it through the bars of the cage, pushing it from side to side. She played with it, taunting it, manoeuvred it and tried to make it sing from the bars of the cage.

A woman watched the girl as she walked and she also observed the condition of the bird in the cage. After a period of watching the girl from a distance, she approached the girl and initiated a conversation.
"What do you have in the cage, little girl?"
I have a bird
"What are you going to do with the bird?"
I will play with it, make it do tricks for me, and make it sing for me.
"What will you do after that?"
When I am tired of it, I will kill it.

The woman looked at the little girl and then asked the question: "Would you let me have the bird in the cage?"

The little girl thought for a while and then said: *You can have the bird in the cage, but you will have to pay a price.*

"I'll gladly pay the price."

The woman paid the price, took the bird, walked with it for a while and then took it to a high place. She opened the cage doors and said: "Bird, you are free! You were not created to live your life in a cage. You were created in the image of God to soar free."

But the bird had been trapped in this cage for a long time and it did not really believe that it was free. It clung to the bars of the cage for security. It was afraid to move towards the open door. The woman understood, and she engaged in a ministry of presence; simply standing with the bird until it was ready to trust her enough to move towards the opened door. She watched as it moved closer and closer and then one day it took the leap, it left the cage. The bird began to fly close to the cage in an unsteady pattern. However, it soon gained confidence and began to fly higher and higher. And, one day it left the area of the cage never to return again. The woman thought she heard the bird chirping as it flew into the sun, "free at last, free at last, thank God almighty, I am free at last."

My first affirmation is that in spite of the fact that Jesse Jackson is running for President of the United States of America; that the Cosby Show (a serial about Black family life in America) is the highest-rated television series in America; that there is an increase in the number of Black faces that are appearing in the world of sports, entertainment, the mass media and even politics; and despite the fact that some Black Americans have entered the middle levels of society – *the systemic and pervasive character of racism in the United States has created a condition of life for the majority of Black Americans that can be compared to the analogy of a bird that is trapped in a cage.*

During 1986 and 1987 racist violence was a fact of life: south and north, east and west:

In Forsyth county, Georgia, a mob of six hundred Whites led by sixty Klansmen attacked and stopped a "Brotherhood March" by seventy-five Whites and Blacks. The mob was hostile, waving confederate flags, screaming racial epithets and holding banners proclaiming "Racial purity is Forsyth's security."

In Howard Beach, New York, a group of White youths attacked a couple of Black people who had stopped at a pizza stand in their neighbourhood. A Black man was killed as he was being chased by the youths into the middle of rush hour traffic.

On the University of Alabama campus in Tuscaloosa, a cross was burned in front of a house into which a Black sorority was thinking of moving. Two white students were arrested, and released.

In Forrest City, Arkansas, a Black employee of the United States Department of Agriculture received a promotion and his home was burned to the ground with a burned cross discarded nearby. An investigation indicated that some of his co-workers were members of the Klan.

In California, Chicano students were harassed and assaulted after Chicanos won election to the student government for the first time.

In Massachusetts, three white men were charged with beating three Vietnamese immigrants whom the police found covered with blood.

In hundreds of other incidents Black people and other people of colour were threatened, assaulted and murdered in their homes, their schools, their places of worship. In most instances the violence was the result of spontaneous activity by people unaffiliated with any white supremacist organization. In other cases the violence was carefully planned by Klansmen and Neo-Nazis with definite political objectives. These hard-core Klansmen and Neo-Nazis formed a clandestine network and launched a guerrilla war in order to terrorize the White majority into submission for the purpose of eliminating their stated enemies. During 1986 and 1987, belated but aggressive action by law enforcement authorities caused several setbacks for this section of the white supremacist movement.

In 1984, a collection of Klansmen and Neo-Nazis formed the so-called Populist Party. The Populist Party developed a multi-planked political platform, raised funds and ran candidates for political office.

However, the most insidious channel that organized white suprema-cists have developed is a phony theology called "Christian Identity". Identity believes and maintains that White northern Europeans are the lost tribe of Israel and that Jews are the result of a mating between the Devil and Eve. Black people and people of colour are considered pre-Adam – a lower bestial form of humanity; and the United States is the Promised Land, the site of the final battle between good and evil or Armageddon.

These persons are fully equipped for the battle. They possess fully automatic assault-rifles, light anti-tank weapons, and land mines. Paramilitary training has supplanted shotguns and deer rifles mounted on the rear windows of pick-up trucks. Unplanned midnight arson and random shootings have been replaced by careful planning and ideologically-chosen targets. Law enforcement officials, judges, media personalities and others of presumed influence have been added to the lists of Blacks, Jews and undocumented workers as appropriate targets.

Christian Identity adherents consider race rather than faith the basis of grace. On its face it appears to be a caricature of itself. But tens of thousands of White Christians have embraced Identity because of its emphasis on scripture and Identity's pseudo–religious wrappings.

As frightening as this movement is, the most viable and painful signs of the cage analogy are in the economic consequences of racism. All the major social indices and numerous statistics show the situation to be worsening, not improving. The gap between White and Black median

family income and employment actually widened in the decade between 1970 and 1980 (even before Ronald Reagan took office). And the Reagan administration has been like an economic plague to the Black community:
  – Black unemployment has skyrocketed;
  – the major brunt of slashed and gutted social services has been borne by Black people especially women and children;
  – the rate of unemployment among Black youth has climbed to 50%.
It is the economy itself that now enforces the brutal oppression of racism. In the changing capitalistic order, manufacturing jobs are lost to cheaper labour markets in the third world or to automation causing farm labour to become extinct; both historically have been important to black survival. In the new "high tech" world and "service economy" almost the only jobs available are at places like McDonalds.

The cold economic savagery of racism has led to further decline in every area of life in the Black community– health, infant mortality, family breakdown, drug and alcohol abuse and crime. The majority of Black children are now born to single mothers; a primary cause of death for young Black men today is homicide and nearly half of all prison inmates in the United States are Black males.

Despite landmark court decisions and civil rights legislation, two-thirds of Black Americans still suffer from education and housing that is both segregated and inferior. Such conditions along with diminishing social services, lead to despair, massive substance-abuse and criminality; and the fact that this reality is still surprising or incomprehensible to many White Americans raises the question of how much racial attitudes have really changed.

My second affirmation is that the church is deeply implicated in maintaining the cage of racism. Martin Luther King, Jr said that America's most segregated hour in the week is at eleven o'clock Sunday morning. It is clear to us that Black people and the Black church have always functioned outside of and beyond white theology and white ecclesiology. The historic exclusion of Blacks by the White church and the emergence of the independent Black church out of that context is integral to what the white church is today in relation to Black people. It is also clearly reflected in what the Black church is about these days. The past isn't simply prologue; it lives in the present.

The Black church emerged as a result of the exclusion of Black people. It sought to serve the interests and needs of an oppressed people living in a hostile environment. The thought, style, worship and practices of the Black church, therefore, cannot be separated from nor fully appreciated apart from the condition in which Black people found themselves.

The church of the Whites continues to support the ideology of white superiority over Blacks. Too little effect is being made by Whites to become conversant with Black culture and Blacks' view of God or the world. The general assumption is that there is nothing worthwhile to be gained from studying Black culture. Whites often believe that they can learn as much as they need to know about Black culture and worldwide views by simply befriending a Black person who has a similar worldwide view and lifestyle.

Whites both inside and outside of the church hold the bulk of economic, political and social power. The whites' inability to relinquish their power and share it continues to reflect the ideology that Blacks are incapable of handling power, that Blacks need to be cared for much as one cares for children and pets, and that Blacks need to have others broker their power for them.

In the past the slave was seen as a labour provider six days a week. Even Sunday morning religious gatherings were not the expression of equals coming together to worship God, rather they were gatherings of those who felt superior but condescending enough to allow an inferior to have access to something which would make him or her a better slave. They also served to alleviate some of the master's guilt about holding persons as slaves in the first place.

The crucial point to remember about those early worship experiences is that the whites were always in control on Sunday, just as they were on every other day. It was the white control of the worship, the inability to accept Blacks as equals, the negation of Black personhood, and the interpretation of scripture and the use of scripture to justify slavery that led to the separation of the Black church from the White church and to the emergence of a Black religious community.

In spiritual and biblical terms racism is a perverse sin that cuts to the core of the gospel message. Put simply, racism negates the reason for which Christ died – the reconciling work of the cross. It denies the purpose of the church: to bring together in Christ, those who have been divided from one another – particularly in the early church's case Jew and Gentile – a division based on race.

There is only one remedy for such a sin and that is repentance which will always bear fruit in concrete forms of conversion, changed behaviour, and reparation.

The church is therefore called to challenge racism in the following ways:

Name It! The church is called to identify racism as a sin against God. We cannot afford to surrender our name, our message and our understanding of the Gospel to those who consider themselves divinely superior. The church is called to position itself in opposition to any force or power that moves contrary to the will of God.

Move from denial to repentance, to conversion and to action.
Whites must examine themselves, their relations, their institutions, for the ugly plague of racism. Whites have benefited from the structure of racism whether they have ever committed a racist act, uttered a racist word or uttered a racist thought. If Whites have profited from a racist

structure they must try to change it. Whites who have accepted Jesus Christ as their Lord and Saviour are called to repentance and conversion.

Stand with the victims of racism! In the face of society's never-ending efforts to deny the basic humanity of Black peoples, the church must clearly come down on the side of those who are most vulnerable. It must extend its name, its resources, its theology, its power and influence to stand with the victims of racism and to join with them in their struggle.

The church must become a political force! The church cannot accept a Christianity that does not relate the message of the gospel to the humanizing of the social, economic, and political structures of the world. The church should encourage and empower persons to participate in the political process.

The church is called to speak to the economic systems under which people exist. How does our faith inform and shape our understanding of the domestic and global economies that we have created? I believe the church should promote reflection and discussion on the relationship between faith and economics, to search for new economic theories and policies more faithful to the gospel.

The church is called to give leadership to the organization of coalitions composed of church leaders, movements of the oppressed and support groups for movements of the oppressed for the purpose of combatting racism.

The church must develop a global perspective. The global perspective enlarges our vision of liberation. What does the church have to say about the fact that two-thirds of humanity is poor and that this poverty and its companion racism arises from the exploitation of the poor nations by the rich nations? In our attempt to liberate ourselves from racism, it is important to be sensitive to the oppressive role of Great Britain and the United States in Africa, Latin America and other third world countries.

Finally, the challenge of the church of Jesus Christ is to proclaim in word and deed a faith that calls for the liberation, redemption and renewal of persons, institutions and nations.

Let me conclude with the second part of the parable I shared earlier in this speech.

One day Jesus of Nazareth was walking the road of life. He encountered Satan who held a cage which contained the souls of men and women. He initiated a conversation.

What do you have, Satan?
"The souls of men and women."
What are you going to do with them?
"I will play with them, manipulate them, coerce them into doing tricks for me, make them sing for me, until I am tired of them."
What will you do when you are tired of them?
"I'll kill them."
Don't kill them Satan. Give them to me.
"I can't give them to you. I bought them. They belong to me. If you want them, you'll have to pay a price."
What's the price, Satan?
"The price is your life."

One day on a cross at Calvary, Jesus paid the price by surrendering his life in order that men and women might live free. On this day in 1987 we who gather here as the Church of Jesus Christ are being called by God to pay the price in order that men and women around the globe who face racism can live as free persons. Some of us, like Martin Luther King, Jr. may be called to pay the price with our lives as we witness for peace and equality in the United States, Great Britian, and the world.

Some of us will be called upon to risk our positions and status as we pressure institutions to change, to become the wholistic and inclusive instruments that God intends.

Let us then, with Jesus Christ at the heart of our efforts and our vision, move to challenge racism. Let us root ourselves in the faith that defines and nurtures us. Let us reach out for the hand of Jesus Christ who is our hope today, tomorrow, and always; for he is the one who is able to make the crooked roads straight and the rough places plain. I am speaking of the God who can make a way out of no way. In the Black religious expression this God has been called a heart-fixer and a mind-regulator.

Sisters and Brothers, with God firmly at our centre, I believe that our struggle for justice and peace will not be in vain. May peace, grace and courage surround each of you as we face the days ahead.

Working Group Reports

*There were nine Working Groups with between eight and twelve people in each.
They met for an introductory session on the Friday night and two main working
sessions on the Saturday. Their written reports were circulated to the rest of the
Conference in time for the Sunday morning plenary. Comments by other
participants were then incorporated into the final reports which now follow. Where
appropriate these reports take the form of firstly recommendations to the Churches
and secondly to Government or other national authorities.*

Working Group A	The Churches and the Programme to Combat Racism
Working Group B	Black Self-help Organisations
Working Group C	Racism in the Church
Working Group D	Employment
Working Group E	Education
Working Group F	Media
Working Group G	Justice, Order and Law
Working Group H	Immigration, Deportation and Sanctuary
Working Group I	Black Theology

Conference Moderators and Speakers

The Churches and the Programme to Combat Racism (PCR)

Addressing the Churches we recommend that –

1   The racism prevalent within the churches, being a reflection of the racism in British society, must be vigorously challenged within the institutional structures. The PCR has an educative and prophetic role to play in support of this process.

2   British churches and related bodies offer platforms for the victims of racism to witness to the support and care mediated by Christ through PCR programmes, and that the PCR be invited to participate in these initiatives.

3   The churches be asked to consider why the PCR programme, much maligned in many UK church and secular circles, is self-evidently "of God" in the estimate of Third World Christians.

4   The insights and recommendations of PCR Consultations (Harare in 1985 and Lusaka in 1987) be studied and implemented, especially as they affirm the role of the liberation movements and the need both to strengthen contacts with them and to promote their Christian content. (The proposed placement of an open letter of support for the ANC by British church leaders is a helpful instance of this process – see Appendix).

5   Churches which reject the PCR's grants from the Special Fund for black liberation movements should consider whether the nature of their perceived problem has more to do with racism than with violence.

6   British churches seek to support the direct promotion of the just cause and the funding of the liberation movements by British church bodies. These initiatives should not in any way reduce the need to give far greater priority within British churches to the funding of the PCR.

Addressing National Authorities we recommend that -

1   As the recent presentation of the ANC as a 'terrorist organisation' by the Prime Minister is neither factual nor helpful, conference participants should write to Mrs Thatcher and say so.

2 In the light of the Prime Minister's statement, Her Majesty's Government be asked to affirm the unquestionable right of the people of Namibia and South Africa to secure justice and peace through the liberation movements.

3 The unrealistic distinction in British charity law between actions which give to the poor (deemed charitable) and actions which strengthen the poor in their pursuit of justice (deemed non-charitable) should be challenged by British aid agencies and Churches.

4 When media presentation of grants from the Special Fund ignores or distorts the humanitarian aspect of the grants, and the fact of their being a response to a South African regime which wages war against its own inhabitants and neighbours, these distortions be repudiated and (where necessary) reported to the Press Council.

Black Self-Help Organisations

All members of this Working Group were Black. By self-help we mean the Black community utilising the resources (human, spiritual, financial and physical) which are available both within and outside our groups, to develop enterprise and activities through extra effort that will contribute to the educational, political, economic and social development of the Black and wider community.

In order to achieve these stated objectives, we see the following as crucial, that the Black community:-

1   needs to develop alterations in the field of education which will make our education system more responsive to the requirements of Black people.

2   needs to develop an approach to social welfare which recognises the cultural background of Black people, for example, the extended family.

3   needs to utilise our resources, actual and political, towards the development of our communities.

4   needs to educate the white community to desist from portraying the Black community as problems and to show that racism is a white problem.

5   needs to be able to take on board the hope and aspirations of all Black youths, recognising that their views are legitimate.

In all the foregoing, the Black-led churches typify the ability of Black people to organise and develop resources in the human, spiritual, financial and physical field, and should be an example to motivate the main-line churches to develop partnership.

Society should be actively encouraged to rise above negative stereotyping and labelling of Black communities and leadership and recognise the strength of unity in diversity.

Racism in the Church

We Need: to learn to respect and value one another
: to address the causes, not just the effects
: to have a vision of the kind of community the church should be
: to change attitudes and structures

Our Education System has a built-in devaluation of black people. The institutional church in Britain as we have come to know it was established by and for white people. The community has now changed but institutions have not and they must be encouraged vigorously to change.

Action

1 There is a vast resource of potential in the black community. That potential needs to be identified and harnessed to contribute to the work of the church and society. The black community must play a major role in ensuring that this happens.

2 Means must be found to increase the representation of black people at all levels in the churches. Quota systems, for all their drawbacks, must be introduced as an interim measure while the processes of education are being changed for both black and white people.

3 Institutions must have an enhanced awareness of equal opportunity practice.

4 Dioceses, circuits, provinces, etc., should establish how many black people are in their congregations and what position they hold.

5 The subject of racism is normally side-stepped and therefore structures to provide the possibility of creatively confronting the issues should be provided. This matter should be a priority particularly in all-white congregations and institutions.

6 Black Christian self-help organisations of young people should be recognised and encouraged.

7 There should be a review of policy and practice for the mutual sharing of the spiritual, pastoral and physical resources of the historic and the black-led churches.

8 It must be made clear to all theological colleges, seminaries and other places of religious learning that the imparting of theology can only be effective against a background of an awareness that we now live in a society that is irreversibly multi-cultural, multi-racial and multi-faith.

There are signs of hope already
Groups of black Christians are increasingly coming into being to discuss, reflect and promote their own concerns.

Employment

We condemn the serious discrimination against Black people in terms of job opportunities, access to capital, training and promotion, and unnecessary obstacles to their employment.

We condemn the failings of the education system and Government schemes such as the Youth Training Scheme and Manpower Services Commission to produce genuine training and job facilities for young people. We are appalled at the extremely debilitating effects of unemployment on communities already under considerable stress, e.g. from bad housing policies, racial attacks, and police harassment, one result of which is severe depression and sickness within the community.

We therefore recommend the following:

To the Churches

1 Capital – We challenge the churches to invest 10% of central funds in Inner City areas to encourage job creation. Dialogue between churches, local community organisations and already existing Black businesses should be initiated.

2 Buildings – There should be urgent clarification of the legal position with reference to the use of church property by schemes creating black employment, with a commitment to lobbying the Charity Commissioners regarding changes to existing laws if deemed necessary.

3 The Church as an employer should be encouraging the implementation of an effective equal opportunities policy and the recruitment of Black people into the church's structures; it should also be carrying out monitoring of the effectiveness of such policies.

4 The Church in the form of the British Council of Churches should approach the Confederation of British Industry (CBI) in relation to the issues of racial discrimination in employment and the high rate of black unemployment to discover what could jointly be done in answer to this problem.

To the Government

1 Greater investment programmes in inner city areas should be undertaken by central Government in partnership with black community organisations, local authorities and private business.

2 A system of contract compliance, equal opportunities and ethnic monitoring should be brought in for the civil service and for all suppliers of goods and services to public bodies. In the meantime the Government should withdraw that part of its Local Government legislation which will limit or inhibit contract compliance as currently practised by local authorities under section 71 of the Race Relations Act 1976.

Education

Widespread debate about the aims and structures of education led to legislation in 1944 based on consensus. Today all provision of education, both formal and informal and at any level, must more adequately reflect the multi-ethnic nature of British society and the challenges and opportunities presented by it. The churches will judge proposals for change on the basis of whether they affirm and reflect the richness of cultural diversity within the community seen in a global context, and whether they address the educational needs of all children. We are particularly concerned at the evidence of continued under-achievement among black and ethnic minority children especially in the inner city.

Recommendations to Government:

For the above reasons we urge Her Majesty's Government to withdraw the current proposals on education in England and Wales and in Scotland, and in particular to reconsider the following points that gave us special concern:

1   The proposals regarding a National Curriculum which reflect a static view of culture and a mechanistic and compartmentalised understanding of education.

2   Teaching methods which are geared to the taking of tests. If these are simply to be used for grading children they will result in greater inequality and reinforce the institutional racism already present in the educational system.

3   The need for subject working-groups to reflect the multi-ethnic and multicultural character of society.

4   The need for Religious Education to be included among any foundation subjects.

5   Greater parental involvement in education needs to be encouraged but free choice for all conflicts with concern for the community's needs. Present proposals offer an illusion of choice for all but in reality introduce the danger of social divisiveness and competition for scarce resources.

Recommendations to the Churches

The Churches should:

1   Participate fully in the national debates on education so as to ensure that legislation is not passed without adequate and fully representative public discussion, not least in relation to the continuance and development of denominational education.

2   Encourage congregations to engage locally in widespread consultation about the educational needs and concerns of the whole community.

3   Examine critically the syllabus and materials used in Religious Education and in their own Christian education programmes in order to eliminate racist concepts and assumptions and to promote racial equality. This should also be done in relation to the programmes and structures of denominational schools and colleges.

4   Consider very carefully the practical, ethical and theological implications of "opting out". This is particularly important for those churches which have their own schools.

Media

The Church should recognise that black people are experiencing continual vilification in press and media against themselves and others fighting for equality and justice. The Church should condemn such practices as morally wrong and socially divisive.

Recommendations to Churches

1   There should be much more black representation at leadership level and on decision-making bodies in the church as a way to educate and influence the media. We do not want tokenism, we want a stone not a pebble. In this context numbers are important; the church must get its own house in order, to be in a position to pick up racism within the media.

2   Christians need to be educated to observe the media objectively and respond as individuals to specific instances of latent racism. Our members need to be encouraged towards letter-writing and telephoning the media, e.g. TV/radio duty officers, phone-in programmes. This would cover news stories, advertising and visual images as well as radio or TV documentaries, etc.

3   It is essential that the local church takes responsibility in encouraging black participation on local radio, in the local press and in any local church press. The local free papers can also be used in this way. There is a need to work, where appropriate, in joint co-operation with black-led churches to influence the media.

4   Local churches should set up groups to monitor the media at local level. Contact may also be made with the local branch of the NUJ to discuss standards of reporting.

Recommendations to Media Authorities

5   There should be more black spokespersons, black leaders, newscasters, reporters and also contributors to "Thought for the Day" and similar spots.

6   There needs to be clear and detailed educational programmes for those working within the media on race issues. One example is the need for an awareness of the effects of language, the use of such words and phrases as blackleg, blackspot, black day, blackmail, black market. Such usage increases identity problems for black people, especially children, which then creates problems for the wider society.

7   Good journalism and positive reporting should be encouraged by all concerned with the media, both within and without. The media is hugely important both as a tool and as an influence. It must be scrutinized, used and exploited as a means of challenging racism.

Justice, Order and Law

As Christians we affirm 'God's undistinguishing regard for all' and see justice as a prerequisite for law and order within our society.

We believe injustice and oppression are the root causes of general alienation and recent disorders. The continuing history of disorders here in Britain highlights the need to pursue measures to tackle injustice, and has sharpened the sense of urgency in the existing search for solutions. We deduce that alienation arises as a result of a denial of rights and resources which in turn is a product of an inherently racist society. Energy should be mainly focused on seeking out underlying causes and getting them put right.

A primary need is the formulation of an equal opportunities policy for all the churches and for society as a whole, especially within the administration of justice and the legislative process.

Recommendations to Churches

1   The British Council of Churches' Executive Committee should call on all member churches and other Christian bodies to devise, implement and monitor equal opportunities policies for their organisations, building on existing initiatives. The development of effective measures of anti-racism procedures, including training, is of crucial importance.

2   Local churches should become involved in effective police-community consultative groups, in nominating Lay Visitors to police stations and in encouraging individual Christians and members of other faiths to become Prison Visitors.

3   The churches must inform themselves of the racist implications of immigration and of criminal justice bills, of the nationality laws, of the proposed community charge and mental health legislation, and the risks in proposals to privatise prisons.

Recommendations to Government

1   We condemn the police oppression of black communities and urge the Government to review police methods of surveillance, arrest, charging, and court sentencing which result in disproportionate numbers of custodial sentences for black people and black prisoners.

2   We recommend the Home Office to ensure that the police increase the protection of black communities from racial harassment and violence.

3   We recommend that the law making racial discrimination a disciplinary offence within the police service be monitored in order to ensure its effectiveness; police training as to what constitutes discrimination is also necessary.

4   We urge the Home Office Prison Department to ensure access as of right to leaders of black-led churches to visit prisoners and as applicants for Prison Chaplaincies.

Immigration, Deportation and Sanctuary

We endorse the view that the whole question of racism in Britain is undergirded by the immigration laws.

We support current British Council of Churches (BCC) policy and in addition make the following recommendations to Church and Government:

Immigration Bill

We call on the churches in alliance with the black communities and people of other faiths:

1 to urge HMG to withdraw the Bill;
2 if the Bill is not withdrawn, to oppose it as yet another example of institutionalised racism;
3 to invite fresh debate towards the formation of a just immigration policy – to this end we call on the Community and Race Relations Unit (CRRU) of the BCC to make suitable material available to enable churches and congregations to campaign on this issue.

Nationality

We call on BCC and all churches to press HMG to remove the time limit on registration for British citizenship, and restore the rights to so register at any time during people's life-time.

Detention Centres

In the light of the current use of detention centres as instruments of deterrence and criminalisation we call on BCC/CRRU to:

1 institute a meeting for airport/port chaplains, immigration advice agencies and campaigning organisations to explore the establishment of appropriate support services for immigrants, migrants and refugees;
2 investigate and challenge the legality of the use of Detention Centres in respect of refugees;
3 urge the appointment of full-time chaplains rooted within the life of local churches to provide support for detainees;
4 encourage local churches to consider the provision of accommodation and bail for detainees.

Legal Services

We call on BCC/CRRU in collaboration with the Immigration Law Practitioners Association to:

1   identify ways of building up the existing networks of advice services,
2   encourage the churches and local congregations to be more aware of the services and resources available;
3   promote greater involvement of churches and local congregations in those networks.

Refugee Policy

We call on BCC in collaboration with other bodies, both nationally and at European level, to explore and campaign against the growing and co-ordinated restrictionism of Western European governments.

Deportations and Sanctuary

Recognising the injustice inherent in the present system of immigration and nationality law and the role that sanctuary is playing in the anti-deportation struggle we call upon:

1   the churches to oppose deportations wherever appropriate, especially where there is personal danger or a threat to family life;
2   the Conference to send a letter of solidarity to existing sanctuaries in Britain;
3   the BCC/CRRU to ask member bodies and other churches to circulate petitions and/or leaflets of existing anti-deportation and sanctuary campaigns through their regular mailings and publications;
4   the BCC/CRRU to prepare an information pack to assist congregations who may consider giving sanctuary.

Definition

Black Theology is a "Word about God" from the perspective of black people of faith. It evolves out of the context of our history, culture, experience, joy and pain.

We offer this as a statement that arises out of our particular situation and we recognise it as a starting-point in a process that must be in dialogue with "Words about God" from other oppressed peoples.

While Black Theology arises out of a particular experience, it nevertheless speaks to the universal condition of people in faith. Black Theology should be informed by an interfaith dialogue which can extend its parameters, enrich its strengths and cement political struggles.

Context of Racism

Out of the insights of the Black-led churches we re-state the truth that racism within the white-dominated church and society has led to the need for the affirmation of Black leadership and a space which affirms Black values and worth.

Dynamic of Black Theology

Affirmation: Black Theology affirms Black people as persons of worth and dignity, created in the image of God.

Revelation: It reveals the hidden mystery of God in our lives who through Jesus Christ is redeeming and healing.

Praxis: It is a motivation for reflection and action that prophetically challenges and transforms society.

Solidarity: It is the impetus for solidarity among and between oppressed people on a global scale.

Our Vision for Black Theology

It is pro-active rather than re-active, subversive rather than superversive; healing and liberating rather than doctrinaire; strategising for action rather than declamatory.

The Way Forward

1 A Grassroots Movement:
– *a broadbased political and theological coalition of forces for justice*
– *a forum to articulate shared concerns and to be the "Black" voice that could still form coalitions to strengthen the case for liberation*
– *a means of dialogue among Black people about preferred and effective strategies for action*

2 A Theological Movement:
– *to develop these ideas for authentic and radical theological expression and action*
– *to initiate a national Black Christian organisation?*
– *to set up centres for training and theological experiment and research aiming to provide Black leadership for Church and Society*

3 Role of CRRU/PCR
– *to challenge the Churches through CRRU/PCR to facilitate the realisation of the above programme.*
– *CRRU is invited to initiate a programme in conjunction with any existing Black Christian groups to enable the meeting and sharing of insights with Black Christians in other parts of the world.*

All Saints Declaration on Racism in Britain

Statement from the Conference on Challenging Racism in Britain, co-sponsored by the Programme to Combat Racism of the World Council of Churches and the Community and Race Relations Unit of the British Council of Churches.
All Saints Pastoral Centre, All Saints Day, 1987

We have met here at All Saints Pastoral Centre over three days, one hundred representatives from the traditional churches and Black Christian organisations, from anti-racist organisations both secular and religious, from the World Council of Churches' Programme to Combat Racism, the British Council of Churches' Community and Race Relations Unit and the Churches' Committee for Migrants in Europe; from all over the United Kingdom as well as from Europe, Asia, Africa and USA. In almost equal numbers we are White and Black, the latter term meaning people of African, Asian or Afro-Caribbean origin including Black people born in Britain. The great majority of us are permanently resident in Britain.

Racism is immoral. We affirm that racial prejudice and discrimination are anathema to people of all religions and all humanitarian ideologies. For Christians racism is sin, rebellion against God, and must be confronted and eradicated from human relationships and institutions. We are all aware of the need for reconciliation across racial barriers in many parts of our world, including Britain, but it is our belief that such reconciliation can only come between peoples engaged in a common struggle for justice, and a shared opposition to racism and determination to root it out. Christians believe that Christ himself if engaged within that most urgent struggle today.

We have acknowledged the existence of racism in today's Britain. We have discussed its causes, and the trends and patterns by which it manifests itself. We have heard from those most affected by racism and those of all peoples, black and white, who are actively engaged in building a successful plural society. We have engaged in mutual criticism and challenge; recognising that racism remains a problem for us Christians in our own organisations.

We see racism present in all our institutions – the law, education, housing, health, media and politics, in the professions, the trade unions and the churches. We see racism present in immigration policies, employment practices, educational materials, press reporting, policing operations and the ways the churches themselves work. We see racism present in the attitudes and policies of those in power in our nation. We see racism present most destructively within the structures of society; therefore, recognising also the damage caused by individual prejudice, we must tackle and eradicate both individual and structural racism.

We call upon the churches – our churches –

● to campaign vigorously against the proposed immigration legislation, to provide accommodation and bail for refugees and asylum-seekers, to oppose deportations wherever appropriate and to support those seeking sanctuary in churches and other places of worship;

● to become involved at national and local level in challenging racism in our penal system. For example as Lay Visitors to police stations, as Prison Visitors, in those police community consultative committees which are effective, in ensuring access for black church pastors and leaders of other faiths to penal institutions and to prison chaplaincies, in encouraging more black magistrates;

● to participate fully in the current educational debate particularly with reference to the implications of a 'national curriculum' and of 'parental choice' for the advancement of a multicultural community;

● to reallocate a significant percentage of church funds to create real jobs in consultation with local black communities and to seek means of offering church property for employment initiatives;

● to increase as a matter of urgency financial support to the World Council of Churches' Programme to Combat Racism and the Projects Fund of the British Council of Churches' Community and Race Relations Unit, asking that churches and individual Christians which reject the PCR's support for the liberation movements because of the issue of violence look again at this matter, not least with regard to the violence of the South African State;

● to adopt effective equal opportunities policies with specific targets, to monitor the numbers of black Christians in the traditional denominations and the positions they hold and thereby to ensure adequate black representation at all levels in the churches;

● to recognise the black-led churches as a powerful witness to the Kingdom of God and as exemplifying the ability of black people to organise also in social, financial and practical ways;

● to offer active support for the growing movement of Black Christians in both black-led and traditional churches to affirm their own identity, to recognise their right to meet, train and organise together and to offer resources for that process;

● to vigorously challenge all racist practices in the media, and commend good and fair reporting where it occurs, in newspapers, radio or TV.

We call upon the British Government –

- to be sensitive to the awareness in all the black communities that present immigration and nationality law is racist and therefore to withdraw the proposed Immigration Bill, to offer amnesty to 'overstayers', to end the use of detention centres for refugees and asylum-seekers and to extend the period of registration for British citizenship;

- to withdraw the projected educational legislation in order to heed representations from the black and ethnic communities and the churches with respect to a 'national curriculum', 'parental choice' and the multicultural character of our society;

- to undertake substantial new investment schemes to create real jobs in inner city areas, in partnership with black community organisations, local authorities and private business;

- to accept the principles of equal opportunities and ethnic monitoring (by an external body) for all public employees and to retain and extend the practice of contract compliance;

- to actively support disciplinary action against police and prison officers practising racial discrimination and harassment;

- to undertake an immediate review of police methods, probation service reporting and court practices which result in a disproportionate number of black people receiving custodial sentences;

- to use its influence to halt the increasingly negative presentations of race issues and the use of racially-biased language in the press and mass media;

- to note the deep anxiety that the linkage of the community charge with the electoral register will lead to the disenfranchisement of many of those in our most deprived areas;

- to affirm the right of the people of South Africa and Namibia to seek justice and peace through their liberation movements and to withdraw immediately the presentation of the ANC as a 'terrorist organisation'.

We commend all these recommendations particularly to Christians in predominantly white areas as it is here that racism, although sometimes hidden, is actually most pervasive.

The Community and Race Relations Unit of the British Council of Churches will seek to encourage the taking up of these Recommendations with relevant church and state bodies and to monitor their effects.

Finally we affirm from our different faith-perspectives:

Our delight in the diversity of the human family

Our conviction that all people of good-will, Black and White, must continue to struggle actively for racial justice

Our belief that there is only one race – the human race – to which we all belong.

November 1st 1987

View from the Base
Interviews with Participants
1: Black People feel Marginalised

Veronica Barnes, from Nottingham, believes that as a Christian and a woman there is a lot for her to do. She came to Britain from Jamaica when she was fifteen and after a varied life on both sides of the Atlantic is now back in Nottingham and is a member of an all-Black Church, the Wesleyan Holiness Church. She is planning to start her own business but still finds plenty of time for church and community.

"In the secular community they tend to put church people down. But we should be fighting for the same things and affiliated with other organisations. God is not a God of separation. He's a God who brings us together. Racism is there but we ourselves as black people have to identify our own ideals and ideology and get what we want out of life. We need to be in touch with other black organisations and groups and find out what can be done together".

Representing UKIDI, a community-linked project to support disadvantaged black groups in Nottingham on issues like education, policing, immigration, deportation and legal and welfare rights, Veronica sees this and other local welfare groups in Nottingham as providing essential help for and by the black community.

But it is hard work. "There's lots going on but also a need for new blood. Most of the people who used to be there battling tend to get creamed off. Those left need to have great commitment to cope with a tremendous amount of work".

Veronica feels that one of the greatest challenges concerning racism rests at the doors of the established churches.

"The established churches make black people feel marginalised. There is no togetherness at all. A lot of people haven't got the power to effect change. The established churches have the resources and funds that could assist black people. Too many wrongs have been committed by them in the past. Slavery went on for four hundred years and yet how many Christian people are involved with the Manpower Services Commission where training is a disgrace. The church has the machinery to do these things well.

"Black people are trying to catch up. But the churches must take a responsibility for why we have not excelled and are still not excelling. People in the churches need to be committed on the issue of racism.

"We need to wipe away the myths. Only when that happens will we get on better."

2: Churches cannot escape their Duty

Benjamin Agwunobi has been working for the Broadwater Farm Defence Campaign in Tottenham, north London, as a researcher for the last 18 months. Previously working in the civil service he was already living in the community and familiar with its problems and successes when serious trouble flared in 1985.

On 5 October Mrs Cynthia Jarrett, a black mother, fatally collapsed during a police raid in her home. The following day violence flared on the Broadwater Farm Estate and PC Keith Blakelock was killed.

Haringey Council called for a public inquiry but the appeal was rejected by the Home Secretary. Although the police refused to participate Haringey Council set up its own inquiry. Lord Gifford was appointed Chairman and with him helping investigate the background to the disturbances were two churchmen, the Rt. Revd Phillip Harvey, nominated by Cardinal Basil Hume, and Canon Sebastion Charles of Westminster Abbey.

The inquiry made a series of wide-ranging recommendations including co-operative policing, a job plan, government funding in line with other deprived boroughs and regular consultations with the community. But for the families directly affected, the nightmare of events surrounding those days is still with them.

Benjamin's committee works with them acting on behalf of those arrested and liaising with their relatives. Of 362 people arrested 157 were charged, and sixty-nine charged with the gravest offences of affray, petrol bombs, riot and murder. Twenty pleaded guilty and of forty-nine who pleaded not guilty twenty-two were convicted. Overall sentences ranged for twelve months to thirty years.

The Defence Committee is concerned at what it sees as a number of cases of miscarriage of justice, inconsistencies and lack of evidence, fanned by sensational press reporting. Following sentences it made some immediate Appeals.

According to Benjamin: "People's civil liberties and rights are being constantly eroded. Arrest methods, intimidation, court sentences. It happens all the time and should shock no-one. People aren't anti-police but they are against unprofessional attitudes adopted by the police as well as policing methods. Some 9,165 police were placed on stand-by just six days after the disturbances.

"We will continue to research, highlight and document what happened that night. We have to help the families morally and legally. The families talk to you for hours about their experiences. They have no-one else to talk to. Neighbours don't understand what it can mean to have relatives serving a long sentence. It adds up to frustration."

Some families were moved off the estate after the disturbances. They wanted to start a fresh life. But they cannot identify with their new areas. "At least Broadwater Farm people still have friends there."

"The struggle is continuing", Benjamin says," in a much more civilised manner nowadays. The police recognise they have blundered in the past and, hopefully, they will not blunder again. It's a problem convincing people that Broadwater Farm is not 'anti-police' but has to contend with a police force which doesn't understand.

"We have lots of volunteers – barristers, solicitors – helping with our research work and lots of non–professional people who volunteer to assist and monitor the families."

The churches have been involved in civil rights issues relating to the Farm and Benjamin is adamant that this should continue. "We want the churches to help us as much as possible. We're dealing with people's lives and with justice. Churches cannot escape their duty here."

Reflections

We asked for participants in the Conference, two white and two black to reflect on the important points of the conference for them. The Revd Brian Beck is the Secretary of the Methodist Conference, The Revd George Wilkie was a Church of Scotland representative and his reflection is excerpted from his report to its Church and Nation Committee; Canon Ivor Smith-Cameron is the Moderator of the Community and Race Relations Unit and Jerome Mack works in anti-racist training for the Unitarian and Free Christian Churches.

Jerome Mack

The salient issue which dominates my impression of the Conference was the absence of a balance between rhetoric and action. Indeed, many of those to whom I spoke voiced concern at the continued "breast-beating" hegemony of the victims juxtaposed against the agonised silence of the majority. Outstanding speeches notwithstanding, I was struck by the similarities of this conference and those I attended during the early days of the American Civil Rights movement. There too, innumerable hours were spent bemoaning personal experiences of discrimination without a concomitant focus on strategies to address or eliminate them.

I was personally delighted with the keynote address by the MP from Brent South, Paul Boateng, who focused our attention on three broad issues, immigration, inner-city legislation, and the need to confront the growing mental health crisis within the black community. An eloquent and impassioned speaker, Mr Boateng epitomised the refrain – young, gifted and black!

Mr Martin Mabiletsa, member of the Johannesburg Bar and the ANC, was equally eloquent in style, and used the interesting technique of comparing and contrasting racism in South Africa with that experienced in Britain, both past and present. His analysis gave cause to doubt our ability to eradicate this problem.

Dr James Mutambirwa gave a scholarly dissertation on PCR funding, or lack thereof, and a scathing indictment of the general unwillingness to contribute towards actions to directly combat racism world-wide.

Last, but not least, we heard an inspiring and loquacious affirmation from Dr Yvonne Delk, of the United Church of Christ, USA, of the need to move from denial to repentance and to take responsibility (especially among white Christians) in standing with the victims of racism through coalitions and economic support.

Ivor Smith Cameron

"Never is an idea more potent, than when its hour has come" This saying is very true about the theme of Racism in Britain, and the PCR Consultation at London Colney was an event of 'kairotic' significance, by which I mean that it took place at the right moment and involved, in general, the right groups of persons, who engaged in reflection and in urging action about the right matters.

Now for some reflections on the Consultation, which must, perforce be personal and so as a result will not be comprehensive. I write as a black person, a priest in the Church of England who has done his share in trying to influence for good the structures of that institution to identify and eradicate the "structural sin" of racism which pervades it, as it does other religious and secular structures in British society.

1. From the outset of the Consultation the scene was set by Paul Boateng MP, who deserves our thanks, support and prayers as he encounters both within and outside Parliament opposition to his statesmanlike, cool, level-headed and imaginatively creative stand against racism in our national legislation, in the areas of housing, prisons, medical care (mental health, for example), employment etc. His opening address produced a climate of black people "coming of age". Yes, there must not be a lack of passion, and even anger, but in the end we have to work together constructively and speak that we might be heard.

The addresses to the Consultation by Yvonne Delk, Martin Mabilesta and James Mutambirwa were all equally splendid and full of profound content and vision. For me at least, all the talks were enriching and transforming.

2. The membership of the consultation was equally significant. It was ecumenical, and the presence of black women and men from the traditional and the Black Churches, and the Roman Catholic Church, was a unique step forward in Christian opposition to racism. They, together with Black activist groups and the 'decision-makers' in the governing bodies of the churches, made an excellent gathering. It was evident throughout the Consultation that no one knew everything, everyone knew something and all listened and learnt from each other.

3. A word about the Working Groups. I can only say that a wide array of themes were dealt with and my Working Group on the theme of 'Racism in the Church' repaid in its recommendations made to the Churches, and to the Government, the seriousness with which all the members of that Working Group listened to each other and together worked out what we believed we wished to say to our churches and our Government. Our recommendations – as indeed were those of the other Working Groups – were concrete, practical and appropriate.

It was a most worthwhile Consultation and another tiny step in Britain towards expressing our deep hope that our society become more human. A good deal of what we were discussing and sharing in words and actions was summed up in prayer and praise and adoration.

Brian Beck

Some have prominence thrust upon them. I had anticipated slipping into the back row of this conference, listening and learning, and perhaps sometimes responding. At the last moment, for unforeseen reasons, I found myself presiding over the opening session and a member of the little circle that had to put together the draft of the conference Declaration from the material supplied by the groups. My reflections are thus more those of a participant in the conference than one of the planners or contributors.

I think I would describe the mood of the conference as "level-headed passion". There was evidence of anger – with so much experience of indignity and pain how could there be no anger? – but there was also a realism about the scale of the problem and the difficulty of addressing it. Those who have recognised the existence of institutional racism are not likely to resort to simplistic solutions. We were immensely helped by the political and legal experience of our speakers and others in the group to distinguish long-term and short-term objectives and identify precise targets.

I was moved also by the dignity of our relationships. No one was present on sufferance, none was patronised and none, so far as I was aware, felt intimidated. So there was an openness about our exchanges which made progress possible. Differences of age, skin colour, culture and past experience were transcended. The conference inspired hope as an image of what society at large might become.

The group work was vital to the process. I can only reflect experience of the one to which I belonged; I imagine others were similar. We could have used twice the time available with profit, but I am satisfied that many of the most important issues were touched on. The disadvantage, inevitably, was that although the whole conference "owned" the findings of each group, we were not party to discussions which led up to them. From our different points of view we recognised the rightness of what was being recommended, but missed the education we would have received if we had been able to share in full conference the experience which was shared in the groups. There was an impressive assembly of wisdom with too little time in which to share it. The best conferences are always so.

We ought perhaps, for our own sake and for those who may read our report, have spent a little longer spelling out what racism is. Prejudice at the individual level is well understood, and prevalent in the church as well as in society in ways that we sometimes refuse to admit. How institutions can be racist is even now less clearly understood, and I suspect there remains some ambiguity in this area which needs to be sorted out. We are still a long way from a situation where the majority in church or society are aware of the prevalence of racism, and part of the educational (and moral) task is to identify what it is we are talking about.

The test of this conference is of course what follows. The cynic will regard it as yet another gathering of enthusiasts with yet another string of campaigning, but ineffective resolutions. My reply to the cynic would be a warning not to underestimate the enthusiasm, or the moral seriousness behind it. We were all committed to challenging racism when we came; otherwise I doubt whether we would have been there. There was commitment also in the adoption of the report and the Declaration. But the test will be whether we, especially those of us who were not there as representatives of campaigning anti-racist organisations, maintain our commitment in the circles to which after the conference we have returned.

George Wilkie

The Conference made it clear from the beginning that we were not just talking about areas of Britain where there is a strong concentration of minority ethnic groups. Racism also exists in areas where there are few Blacks and Asians. Racism is an affront to God who created us all. It is present not only in individuals but in institutions and structures. It is an instrument of oppression even when there is no violent action involved.

The programme of the Conference was very full and the atmosphere at times highly-charged. For the black delegates and for many of the Whites who have lived with this problem, racism is the great issue of the day, and attacking racism wherever it is found is a full-time crusade.

The situation of the people with an African or Afro-Caribbean background dominated the debates rather to the exclusion of the Asians – though the presence of one vocal Scottish Muslim (complete with strong Glasgow accent!) did not go unnoticed, nor did the significant difference between the situation of African or Afro-Caribbean communities with a mainly Christian background and that of the Asians with few Christians and many with deeply-held Muslim or Hindu beliefs.

While the tone of the debates tended to be unremittingly critical of British society – Government, police, teachers, churches – there were some who saw signs of improvement and hope in the present situation, especially a middle-aged black woman Pastor from a congregation in Brixton who spoke of a slowly-improving situation in that area. There was perhaps too little self-criticism around. It is not a healthy position for Christians to be in, always to be able to point to the sins of others without self-examination to see if the seeds of such sins also exist in ourselves.

I participated in the working group on the World Council of Churches' Programme to Combat Racism. The black members of our Group were particularly outraged by Mrs. Thatcher's description a few weeks earlier of the ANC as "terrorists", rather than seeing them as freedom-fighters for their people. Their outlook could best be understood by white British people by seeing it as similar to those who opposed Hitler in Germany. They feel that the oppression of black people in South Africa is similar to that of the Jews in Germany. There, the Church failed to resist by and large. The few who did (Bonhoeffer for example) found themselves involved in violence, not willingly, but as part of the struggle against monstrous injustice, oppression and killing. Such people evoke our admiration so why not those who stand against a similar oppression in South Africa? The amount given to the ANC from the PCR last year was about $84,000, "hardly enough to keep an American middle-class family going for a year". And yet to those involved its effect is far greater than the actual amount, "three hundred million Protestants are saying, 'We support you'". We do need to listen to reasonable and articulate black Christians to appreciate how they see their struggle as rooted in the Bible and its story of the human struggle for freedom from injustice and oppression.

Worship was an integral part of the gathering and it was challenging from a white point of view to see how naturally all the concerns of the debates were spontaneously "taken to the Lord in prayer" in the worship sessions. We have a good deal to learn from black Christians in spiritual as well as in more temporal matters.

Epilogue

By the time this Report is published, in April 1988, and read sometime later than that, much will have happened. Some of its urgent recommendations may well have been swept aside – although they were made known to authorities who could have responded. The Government may have made its Immigration Bill law, removing the right of family unification, limiting some people's rights of appeal and reducing entry rights of Commonwealth citizens while affirming those of Europeans. The 'contract compliance' issue may have been resolved by the Government allowing local authorities to ask their contractors questions on equal opportunities so tame as to be effectively useless. The Education Bill may be close to becoming law without any of the suggested rethinking about multi-cultural education, the national curriculum, local government power or the results of parental choice.

But although these matters may date the Report they may also remind us of the kind of intransigence met by so many suggestions and anxieties expressed over national policies in late 1980s Britain. They may be seen as battles fought and lost. They may also be remembered as signposts which pointed another way as those possessing political and economic power strode purposefully the path of arrogance and division. When previously could a gathering of such positive, creative, like-minded people – the great majority Christians representing the full spectrum of British churches – have found themselves so fully behind recommendations so contradictory to the direction of state power?

It may well be that Black Christians in Britain needed this Conference, its Report and Declaration, to see where they stand and why. To confirm that they know where they are going and Who is going with them. But it may also be that White Christians need it more, and not only those who attended but those who could not, and perhaps would not have done even if they could. For all Christians need the Word of God, and it was spoken at All Saints, in terms of the judgements on the injustice within our society, the challenge to its racism, the power of the Spirit manifested by those in the struggle and the joy of repentance shown by sinners glimpsing a little more light.

Hopefully this Report will colour the churches in suburb, village and commuter town, as well as urban priority area and inner city. For the gift of sunlight through the rain, the bow of God's covenant, is for all to receive and all to celebrate. We all need rainbows.

D.H.
March 1st 1988

Support for the ANC

Dear Sir,

We congratulate the African National Congress (ANC) on the occasion of its 75th anniversary year. It has held firmly to a great objective through a period of growing crisis in Southern Africa. It has stood for the basic human and civic rights of all South African people, and the development of a unitary state to which people of all the racial groups may belong.

For the greater part of this long history the ANC's policy was peaceful protest and persuasion, but this made very little impact on the white minority. The ANC was prohibited from taking part in normal activity. The South African authorities adopted increasingly strong measures to silence its leadership, by imprisonment and by exile. After the banning of the liberation movements in 1960, the ANC adopted a policy of meeting the armed violence of the apartheid regime with force, a "just war" about which Christians are divided.

We remain committed to peaceful means of bringing about change. We recognise, however, that it is the policy of the South African regime to control by force a large proportion of its own people and to destabilise its neighbours by military action. This has led the ANC to adopt force along with other means to end oppression.

The international community has failed to offer effective non-violent means of exerting pressure on the South African authorities, despite repeated church urging in western nations.

British churches have participated in the worldwide call for the release of Nelson Mandela and other political prisoners, the unbanning of the liberation movements and the introduction of a democratic political process in which all can equally share. As representatives of British churches we are convinced that the cause of the ANC is just. We support that cause.

We too believe that racial origins must not be used to determine the right to equal treatment and equal responsibility in the national life.

We acknowledge and give thanks for the tenacity and courage of the ANC. It continues to represent a very wide spectrum of South African opinion. We urge our Government to increase contact with its leadership. We pray that reason, Christian teaching, human caring and vigorous political and economic action within the international community may contribute to the day when apartheid is abolished.

Yours Sincerely,

The Rev B. G. THOROGOOD   The Rev PHILIP MORGAN
Chairman, Executive Committee   General Secretary
The British Council of Churches, London, SE1   14 December

Letter to the Independent, Wednesday 16th December 1987

*   *   *   *

Glossary

ANC	– African National Congress	PAC	– Pan Africanist Congress
BCC	– British Council of Churches	PCR	– Programme to Combat Racism
CRRU	– Community and Race	PSI	– Policy Studies Institute
	Relations Unit	SWAPO	– South West Africa People's
GLC	– Greater London Council		Organisation of Namibia
HMG	– Her Majesty's Government	WCC	– World Council of Churches
NEB	– New English Bible		